LIVING IN THE UNITED STATES

Living in

the

United States

by Ani Hawkinson
and Raymond C. Clark

Seventh Revised Edition

PRO LINGUA ASSOCIATES

Pro Lingua Associates

P.O. Box 1348
Brattleboro, Vermont 05302 USA
Webstore: www.ProLinguaAssociates.com
802-257-7779   Orders:800-366-4775
Orders@ProLinguaAssociates.com
SAN 216-0579

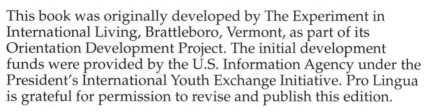

ISBN 0-86647-153-7

This book was originally developed by The Experiment in International Living, Brattleboro, Vermont, as part of its Orientation Development Project. The initial development funds were provided by the U.S. Information Agency under the President's International Youth Exchange Initiative. Pro Lingua is grateful for permission to revise and publish this edition.

The staff of the original development project were: Ani Hawkinson, writer; Alvino Fantini, director; Julie Soquet, project and orientation director; Joy Wallens, production.

Peter deJong, former Secretary General, and the Directors of the various Experiment in International Living National Offices identified the original content areas covered in this country-specific series.

Since the second edition, the writers and editors have been Raymond C. Clark and Arthur A. Burrows.
Many revisions and additions made in the fourth and later editions were suggested by David P. Rein and Edgar Sather.

Designed and set by Judy Ashkenaz of Total Concept Associates in Brattleboro, Vermont, using Palatino text and Mistral display types.
Cover design by Arthur A. Burrows.
Cover illustration by Maisie Crowther. Printed by Sheridan Books of Fredericksburg, Virginia.

Seventh, revised edition for 2002
Printed in the United States of America

Living in the United States

Lincoln Memorial

The first Thanksgiving
1621

Contents

3. Country Facts   42

Appendix: The 50 States   67

JEFFERSON MEMORIAL

Special Note

In this book we have used the terms *America* and *American* to mean "the United States" and "citizen of the United States." We are aware that people from the other Americas are also Americans. But unfortunately there are no other single words in the English language at this time that can be used in place of "America(n)."

1. First Steps

This section of the book will help you learn how to live in the United States. We will give you the basic facts about life in the United States, but every state, city, and town will be a little different. You will need to find the differences and the details. For example, we can tell you about restaurants in the United States, but you must find the places that have food that you like. We can tell you about transportation in the United States, but you must find the best way to go from place to place in the town where you live. We can make suggestions, but you must make the final choices. Good luck!

1.1 Money and Banks

The **dollar** is the currency of the United States. There are 100 cents in a dollar. American money comes in the following denominations: 1, 5, 10, 25, 50 cent coins, and the Sacagawea dollar coin. There are also Eisenhower silver dollars and Susan B. Anthony dollar coins, but they are very rare. In paper money, there are 1, 2 (not common), 5, 10, 20, 50, and 100 dollar bills. There are larger dollar bills, but they are not used in everyday life.

Be careful with American bills. They are all the same size and color. They have recently been redesigned, so you may find two different designs for any bill.

American **coins** have special names which you need to know. They are:

1 cent	—	a penny
5 cents	—	a nickel
10 cents	—	a dime
25 cents	—	a quarter
50 cents	—	a half-dollar

It is a good idea to carry some change (coins) because you may need exact change for certain services, such as parking meters, telephones, and buses (see sections 1.6, 1.8, and 1.9). You may also find that large bills ($50, $100) are not accepted at small stores. You should not carry a large amount of cash. Buy dollar **traveler's checks** before you leave home, or bring an internationally recognized credit card. They are acceptable almost everywhere.

Nowadays Americans use **credit cards** for many of their purchases. You will need a credit card if you want to rent a car. You can pay with cash or traveler's checks when you return the car, but you cannot take the rental car without a credit card. Some hotels also require a credit card when you register. There are many good credit card companies, but MasterCard and Visa are the most common and widely accepted ones.

If you bring your own currency with you, you may change it at a large international airport. You can also change it at a bank. It is not always easy to change your currency at banks in small towns. It is usually better to bring dollars with you. When you arrive at an international airport such as JFK in New York, you may need one-dollar ($1) bills to rent a baggage cart. Porters are not available before you clear customs, so you must carry your own baggage.

Banks in the United States tend to be local and regional. For example, Citibank is one of the largest American banks, but it does not have branches throughout the United States. For this reason, a checking account with a local bank is not useful outside your hometown — except for paying by mail. However, if you are going to stay in one place for a month or more, you may want to open an account at a local bank. It is very easy to do.

Banks are usually open from 9:00 A.M. to 5:00 P.M. and on Friday until 6:00 P.M. They are not open on weekends or holidays (see section 2.14). Most banks offer savings and checking accounts. There is usually a fee for checking accounts, but if you keep a minimum balance (usually about $500), the bank may pay you interest. Banks also offer the **ATM** (Automatic Teller Machine) service. With your ATM card you can deposit and withdraw money at any time at the automatic teller machine and use ATMs all over the country. There are charges for this service.

2

1.2 Food

Americans usually eat three meals a day — breakfast, lunch, and dinner (see section 2.11). Certain kinds of food are typical at each meal. Throughout the United States, the food is similar, but there are some regional differences. In general, American food is plain and not spicy.

One of the most popular American foods is the **burger**. Hamburgers are made of beef, not ham. They are served in a round piece of bread called a bun. They are often eaten with one or more of the following: tomato, lettuce, onion, mustard, and ketchup. A hamburger with melted cheese on top is called a cheeseburger. Some restaurants have other kinds of burgers with other names, such as "jumbo burger" (very big), "mushroom burger," "veggie burger," or "bacon burger." If the menu doesn't explain the different kinds of burgers, ask the waiter for help.

Hot dogs (also called "franks" or "frankfurters") are a kind of sausage. They can be steamed, boiled, or grilled. They are served in a long bun with mustard or ketchup or pickle relish. Hot dogs are often made from pork — the meat from pigs. (Bacon and ham are also meat from pigs.) If you want to avoid pork, all-beef and turkey hot dogs are generally available.

Americans eat a lot of **sandwiches** — especially for lunch. They are made with two pieces of bread and a filling. Some common fillings are tuna fish, egg salad, ham, chicken, turkey, roast beef, cheese, and peanut butter and jelly. Some sandwiches are hot — for example, a hot roast beef sandwich. Another special type is the club sandwich, which is made with three pieces of bread and two fillings between the three pieces. The fillings are often chicken or turkey and ham with lettuce and tomato. Sandwiches made with pita bread are called pockets or wraps, and sandwiches made with a long, round bread are called grinders, subs (submarines), hoagies, or heros. They are very popular.

Pizza is another food eaten in all parts of the country. A large, flat piece of bread is typically covered with tomato sauce and cheese and then baked. Pieces of meat and vegetables are often sprinkled on top of the cheese.

For main dishes — especially for dinner — Americans eat a lot of red meat, although today people are eating more fish and poultry than they used to. Beef is the most popular meat, followed by pork and lamb. In a few places you can find rabbit meat, but you will not find horse, goat, or dog meat. There are many kinds of beef. Hamburger (ground beef) and beef steak are the most common. In general, Americans like thick steaks. There are three ways to cook meat: rare (not cooked very much), medium, and well done (cooked a lot).

Pasta is popular all over America. Spaghetti with a meat or vegetable sauce is often a main dish. Noodles of many kinds are served as side dishes. Macaroni and cheese is very popular.

Salads are often served with a meal. They are eaten before or with the main dish. A salad can also be a main dish — especially for lunch. There are many kinds of salad, but some of the most common ingredients are lettuce, tomato, onion, and cucumber. A kind of sauce called a **salad dressing** is poured on the salad. There are many different kinds of dressings, but the most common types are Italian (oil, vinegar, spices, and herbs), Thousand Island (mayonnaise, ketchup), French (oil, vinegar, mustard, tomato), and Blue Cheese. Some restaurants have their own dressing, which is called the "house dressing." Many restaurants offer a **chef's salad**, which is a large salad — a full meal. In addition to vegetables, it usually contains small pieces of chicken, turkey, ham, and cheese. One other kind of salad, made from cabbage and served in a creamy dressing, is called **cole slaw**.

America's favorite vegetable is the **potato**. It is served in many different ways, but the most common are baked potato (a whole potato cooked in an oven), mashed potatoes (boiled potatoes mixed with milk and mashed into a puree), and French fries and potato chips (strips and slices of potato fried in a deep pot of oil). In a restaurant, you may be asked to choose which kind you want (see section 1.3).

Corn is a truly American vegetable (it can also be called a grain, like wheat and rice). It was grown by Native Americans before the Europeans came to the Americas. Although canned or frozen corn can be found all year, the best time to eat fresh corn is

4

in the summer (July and August). It is especially popular to eat the kernals of corn off of the whole ear (cob) holding the ends with your fingers. This is called "corn on the cob."

Pasta, bread, potatoes, and corn are all starches. Americans generally eat some meat, a starch, and green or yellow vegetables at dinner. They may eat a green salad or a hot vegetable. Popular vegetables found throughout the United States are peas, beans, carrots, lima beans, broccoli, cauliflower, brussel sprouts, squash, spinach, and cabbage. Other vegetables are popular regionally. In general, most vegetables are boiled, but in recent years many Americans are finding new ways to prepare and serve vegetables–steaming and stirfying, for example. Many people have decided to become vegetarians, meaning they do not eat meat. Vegans do not eat meat or dairy products.

For **breakfast**, some Americans eat only bread, some kind of fruit (most often orange juice), and coffee or tea. The bread is usually heated and is called toast. Another kind of breakfast bread is the **donut** (also spelled "doughnut"), a sweet, round piece of fried bread with a hole in the middle or a filling. Another kind of bread often eaten at breakfast is the **bagel**. It looks like a donut, but it is not sweet; it is first cooked in water and then baked in an oven. Some shops specialize in donuts or bagels.

Many Americans eat **cereal** for a quick breakfast. Cereals are made from wheat, oats, rice, or corn, and there are many different kinds. Those that are brightly colored and sweetened are especially popular with children. Cereal producers spend millions of dollars to persuade children and parents that their cereal is exciting and tasty. People serve cereal with milk and sometimes fruit.

When Americans take the time for a bigger breakfast, they often eat **eggs** (fried, boiled, or scrambled) with bacon, sausage, or ham. **Pancakes, waffles**, and **French toast** (bread soaked in egg and milk and then fried) are also popular for bigger breakfasts. They are generally served with a sweet syrup, often maple flavored.

Americans also eat between meals, and these foods are called **snacks**. Generally, snacks are not very nutritious. Chocolate and other candies, potato chips and corn tortilla chips, and cookies and sweet pastry are all very common. This kind of food is called "junk food."

The **fast food** industry has had an important influence on what and how Americans eat. McDonald's, the leader in this industry, is now known throughout the world. McDonald's has made the American hamburger famous. One reason is that in every McDonald's the food is exactly the same and is cooked in exactly the same way. In addition to the nationally known burger chains (McDonald's, Burger King, and Wendy's), other famous fast food restaurants specialize in chicken (Kentucky Fried Chicken), Mexican food (Taco Bell), donuts (Dunkin' Donuts), and pizza (Pizza Hut, Domino's, Little Caesar's).

Although the fast food industry has restaurants in every American town, there are also local and regional differences in American food that you should look for wherever you live or travel. The differences and specialties are too numerous to mention in this small book, but you can find them. Ask, look, and explore.

1.3 Restaurants

Fast food restaurants are the same everywhere in the United States. Local restaurants offer more variety. Here are some general types to look for. **Family restaurants** are good places to bring children. The food is not very expensive and is probably typically middle-class American. These restaurants may not serve alcohol, so if you like a glass of wine or beer with your meal, ask before you sit down (see section 1.4).

6

In **cafeterias** you walk through a line, choose your food, put it on a tray, pay at the end of the line, and carry your food to an empty table. The food is usually inexpensive, and it is ready to eat.

Other informal places to eat are called cafes, coffee shops, sandwich shops, delis (a kind of sandwich shop), diners, and truck stops. While driving along America's highways, you may find it interesting to stop at a truck stop and listen to the conversations of the long-distance truck drivers. Steak houses and seafood restaurants are often more formal and expensive, but they are very common.

Here are a few things you should know about American restaurants:

- Some restaurants have both smoking and non-smoking sections, but many do not allow smoking. Ask before you smoke.
- Many restaurants post menus in the window so you can see the prices before you enter. If they do not, it is acceptable to enter the restaurant and ask for a menu before you sit down, If it is too expensive, it is O.K. to leave.
- At many restaurants, lunch is less expensive than dinner.
- Bread and butter and water are usually served free with the meal.
- If you do not eat all your food you may ask for a "doggie bag." The waiter will put your uneaten food in a bag, and you can take it home.
- The charge for service is not included in your restaurant bill, usually called "the check."
- To ask for the check, signal the waiter with your eyes or a raised hand. If that doesn't work, you can say, "Excuse me," quietly when the waiter comes near you. Then say, "May we have the check, please?"
- You must calculate the tip. The normal amount is 15%. If the service is poor, you may leave less.

- There is usually a food tax added to your restaurant bill. The amount varies from state to state.
- Waiters or servers will be both men and women.
- In some restaurants, waiters have helpers called bus boys. They set tables, bring bread and water, and clear away used plates, but they cannot take orders.

It is common in the United States to find signs saying "PLEASE WAIT TO BE SEATED" when you enter a restaurant. This means you must wait near the sign until someone comes to show you to your seat. The wait is not usually very long. If the restaurant is crowded, you may be told there will be a wait and be asked for your name. Then you will be called by name when there is a place for you. If this happens, be sure to ask how long the wait will be before giving your name. You don't have to stay if you don't have the time. If the restaurant is not crowded, you may see a sign that says, "PLEASE SEAT YOURSELF."

In restaurants, you should be prepared to answer some questions. Here is a list:

- Do you want smoking or non-smoking?
- Would you like something to drink (a cocktail) before you order?
- *(At breakfast)* How do you want your eggs? (soft-boiled, scrambled, poached, fried either sunny-side-up or over-easy, or in an omelet)
- What kind of toast do you want? (white, wheat, or rye)
- What kind of dressing do you want (for your salad)? (see section 1.2)
- How do you want your steak? (rare, medium, or well done)
- Baked, mashed, or fries? (potato)
- Would you like some dessert?
- Regular or decaf (coffee)?
- Do you want your coffee black or with cream and sugar?
- *(In fast food restaurants)* Is that for here or to go?
- How's everything? Is everything all right? *(Waiters usually ask this to see if you need anything and if your food is OK.)*

8

In large cities you can find a wide variety of ethnic restaurants. In small towns you may also find some special ethnic restaurants, depending on the nature of the local population. If there are Thais or Polish people in the community, you may find a Thai or Polish restaurant. All over the United States from big cities to roadsides in the country, you will find Chinese, Italian, and Mexican restaurants. Indian, Japanese, French, and German are also common in some parts of the country.

Many restaurants have a counter at which customers can sit and eat. Many other restaurants have a bar at which customers can sit while drinking alcohol. There are almost always bottles of alcohol showing on the wall behind the bartender at a bar. Often it is possible to get food with alcohol at a bar. Children may always sit at a counter where only food is served, but in most of the country it is not appropriate for children to sit at a bar. Some good restaurants specialize in serving locally made beer. These may be called breweries or pubs, and yet they are appropriate for children who sit with adults at a table. However, bars, pubs, or breweries which are mostly for drinking alcohol will usually not allow children to enter, and women who are alone may want to avoid them.

1.4 Drinking and Smoking Laws

There is a law in the United States that prohibits people under the age of 21 from drinking or buying any alcoholic beverage ("drink"). When you buy or order an alcoholic drink, you may be asked to show proof of your age. You must be 21 or over. You will need a photo-ID (identification card), such as a passport or a driver's license. You will not be allowed in bars and discotheques if you are under 21. You may be stopped at the entrance and asked to show your ID. Bar owners can lose their license to serve alcoholic beverages if they serve alcohol to minors (people below the legal drinking age).

You should also be aware that there are very strict laws against drinking just before or while driving a car. In some places it is illegal to have an open can or bottle of alcohol in a car.

In some places there are laws that control the place or time when alcohol can be drunk or served. For example, in some places alcohol cannot be sold on Sunday. In some public places (beaches, parks), you cannot drink alcohol. Be careful.

Smoking is now prohibited in most public places. Look for signs. If you are not sure, ask somebody. Smoking also is not acceptable in many private homes. In most places, you must be 18 to purchase cigarettes.

1.5 Hotels

In the United States, **motels, inns,** and **hotels** are similar. The main difference between them is the type of building and location. Motels were originally built along highways in the United States to serve long-distance travelers. They are often only one or two stories high and are long narrow buildings where you can park your car right in front of the room you are staying in. They are often found outside of the center of town. Hotels and inns are often larger, more formal and expensive and offer more services.

Hotels and motels are not required to post rates, so it is a good idea to ask when you check in (arrive and register). In a typical room you will find: two single or double beds or a king sized bed (you can usually request what you want), a telephone (sometimes with a computer connection) and telephone directory, a private bathroom with towels and soap, a television, individually controlled heating and air conditioning, a closet for your clothes and luggage, a Bible, writing supplies (paper, envelopes, and postcards), electrical outlets, drinkable tap water, glasses, and usually a container for ice (an ice bucket; the ice can be obtained from machines located in various places throughout the building). In addition, many hotels provide a directory of the services provided, such as room service (you telephone an order for food to be delivered to your room) and overnight laundry service. Most hotels have smoking and non-smoking rooms or floors. Most Americans now feel strongly that you should not smoke in a non-smoking area.

Breakfast usually is not included in the room rate. Most hotels and motels have their own restaurant and/or coffee shop where you can obtain meals, but you must pay in addition to the cost of your room. This is also true of room service. In both cases, you may charge everything to your room number and pay for it when you leave. Room service is more expensive than eating in the hotel coffee shop or restaurant.

You should also be aware of two additional hotel/motel expenses. The cost for using the telephone in your room is often very high. It is usually much cheaper to use a pay phone (see section 1.6) or your own calling card. Motels do not have people to help you with your luggage, but hotels do. They are called "bell-hops," and they expect a tip. One dollar ($1) for each bag is acceptable.

11

Less expensive places to stay are **youth hostels** and **YMCAs/ YWCAs** (Young Men's/Women's Christian Association). You do not need to be a "youth" or a "Christian" to stay in a youth hostel or a YMCA/YWCA; all you need is a pass, which you can obtain in your own country or at a hostel in the United States. Hostels provide simple dormitory sleeping arrangements with a community kitchen. You can obtain information in the *Hostel Guide and Handbook* published annually by American Youth Hostels. Write to 20 West 17th Street, New York, NY 10011. Most YWCAs and YMCAs have overnight accommodations, and they are usually centrally located in large cities. Their rates are about half those of hotels, and both members and non-members are welcome. They are referred to informally as *"the Y,"* and usually have a swimming pool, gymnasium facilities, and sometimes cultural and social events.

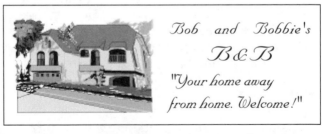

Bob and Bobbie's

B&B

"Your home away from home. Welcome!"

In recent years, another kind of hotel is becoming popular. It is called a **bed and breakfast** or B and B, and it is similar to the European *pension*. The building is actually a large private home that has been converted to a small inn for overnight visitors. Staying in a bed and breakfast will bring you in close contact with local people. Tourist offices or the local Chamber of Commerce in most towns will have listings of B andB's.

1.6 Telephone

One of the best guidebooks for you will be the **Yellow Pages** in the telephone directory ("telephone book"). You will find almost every kind of service listed in the Yellow Pages — for example, restaurants, hotels, travel agents, banks, schools, medical centers, automobile repair, etc., etc.

Coin-operated public telephones, called **pay phones**, can be found almost everywhere: gas stations, hotel lobbies, transportation terminals, restaurants, malls, shopping centers, city sidewalks, and public areas. To use one, you will need thirty-five cents in coins for most local calls. The phone will not give change, so if you do not have exact change, do not expect to get anything back from what you put in. If you are paying for the call with coins, the operator will check to make sure you have enough change before the call is put through. Your call will be interrupted by a recording telling you to put more money in if you have used up the time allowed by your initial deposit.

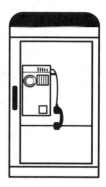

If you don't want to pay for a call with coins, you can **charge** it or place your call **collect**. This is common practice on long-distance calls. If you call collect, the person you are calling will have to pay for the call by "accepting the charges."

In order to place a collect call or to charge one, or to call **person-to-person** (when you pay only if the person you ask for comes to the phone), you must dial 0 (for "operator") and then the number you are calling. You will hear a chime, and then an operator will come on the line. If you are calling collect, the operator will ask the person who answers your call if they accept the charges. If you need to charge a call to a number other than the number you are calling, you can ask the operator and he or she will do so if there is someone at that number to accept the charge.

Many people who travel or want to place personal calls from phones other than their own, have **calling cards** (telephone credit cards). Before coming to the United States, call your local telephone company and ask if you can get a calling card you can use in the U.S. and have the bill sent to your home.

To use a calling card, you need to know if the phone you are using has a round rotary dial or push buttons and, if it has buttons, whether it is a "touch-tone" phone (on which each button makes a different dialing sound) or a "pulse" phone (on which the tones are all the same). If you are using a touch-tone phone, after you dial 0 and the number and hear the chime, you enter your calling card number using the buttons. If you are using a rotary dial or pulse phone, after the chime an operator will come on the line to get your calling card number.

Recently, a new kind of phone has been installed which is designed only for calling card callers. These phones do not take money, and you cannot use them unless you have a calling card. In some cases, you can pass the magnetic strip on your calling card through a slot on the phone, or you may be able to use the buttons. These phones are usually found in airports where regular, coin-operated phones are also located.

You can also buy prepaid calling cards. You buy a certain amount of minutes with the card. With many cards, you can buy additional time and have it added to your card. They are easy to use and not expensive.

Cellular phones have become popular in the United States as they have in other countries. You may want to get a cellular phone for convenience if you will be staying in America and traveling. Calls will be billed to your account.

Many businesses offer an **800** number. This means it does not cost you money to call them. To use this service, first dial 1, then 800, 866, 877, or 888, and then the seven-digit number. Other companies offer services using a 900 number. These services are generally information and entertainment, and the cost is charged to your phone bill. These services are often very expensive.

Telephone numbers are preceded by a three-digit **area code** number, which generally is different from state to state. Most states have more than one area code number. One useful number is 1 plus the area code plus 555-1212. This is for **directory assistance** — to find a telephone number you don't know. If you are dialing for a telephone number within your own area code, you dial 1-555-1212. In some places, you can save money by dialing 411 to reach directory assistance for local numbers.

In an emergency when you need the police, fire department, or an ambulance, you can dial **911** for free from most places in the United States. In some places this will put you in touch immediately with the police. In other places, 911 will reach a special operator. You can, of course, simply dial 0 to reach a regular operator but that takes a little more time. Saving a few minutes can make the difference between life and death in some emergencies.

Also remember that there are four time zones in the United States, so there is a three-hour time difference between New York and California. (9:00 A.M. in New York is 6:00 A.M. in California). Check the telephone book for the time difference to the place you are calling.

1.7 Mail, Telegrams, Faxes, and E-mail

Post offices in the United States are usually open from 8:00 A.M. to 5:00 or 6:00 P.M., Monday through Friday, and until noon on Saturday. They are closed on national holidays. You can purchase stamps at any post office, as well as at hotel desks and from coin-operated vending machines located in transportation terminals. Postal rates are based on weight and destination and are changed from time to time, so you should check the cost of mailing letters and postcards when you arrive.

Letters can be mailed at a post office or in red, white, and blue mailboxes located on many street corners in American cities. There is a sign on each mailbox which states the time when the mail will be taken from the box, so you can check to see when your mail is actually going out.

If you want to receive mail while traveling, it can be sent to you c/o General Delivery, Main Post Office, in the town where you expect to be. All general delivery mail must be picked up by you in person, and you will be asked to show identification.

The usual form for a mailing address is:
Name
House or apartment number and street
City, state, ZIP code number

The ZIP **code** number is important. If you don't know it, you should ask at a post office. They will give you the number.

Packages can be sent from any U.S. Post Office using parcel post. There are also special Post Office rates for library mail and printed matter, but it is illegal to include personal letters in these packages. United Parcel Service (UPS) also handles packages. UPS Ground service is sometimes more expensive than the Post Office, but the packages are insured and trackable. UPS will also pick up packages at your residence for an additional charge.

There are several **express services** that offer overnight service for letters and packages; Federal Express, the Post Office's Express Mail, and UPS are the largest. These carriers also offer a less expensive second-day delivery. They are very reliable and fast. Look in the telephone book for phone numbers and addresses.

Telegrams are not sent at the post office as they are in many other countries. The most common way to send one is to make a phone call to Western Union. In general, telegrams are not used very much for communication inside the United States. They are used for money transfers.

Sending information by **fax** is now very common. You can do this at a shop that specializes in printing and photocopying. Many people now communicate on the Internet using **e-mail**. This is the fastest, least expensive way to send a message to someone who uses a computer with a modem.

1.8 Transportation

For traveling in the United States between states and cities, there are four basic ways: plane, train, bus, and car. Each way has advantages and disadvantages. **Air travel** between major cities is, of course, the fastest way. Domestic air travel is generally expensive. However, less expensive fares are often available on special "shuttle" flights and as promotions. Travel agents can suggest the least expensive flights. Many people make their reservations "on-line," meaning through the internet.

The national passenger railway system is called **Amtrak**. For seeing the countryside in comfort, this is the best way to travel. But it is also expensive for longer trips. Sometimes special rates are available for tourists.

Buses are cheaper than planes and trains, and buses go to many more places. Riding for a long distance in a bus, however, is not so comfortable.

Driving a **car** is definitely the easiest way to travel because you can leave, stop, and go when you want. It can also be the cheapest if you share your expenses with other people. The highway system in the United States is very well developed. The **Interstate Highway System** allows you to travel across the entire country without stopping for traffic lights. There are rest areas and restaurant/gas station areas all along the Interstates. The maximum legal speed in the U.S. is 65 miles per hour, but on many highways the speed limit is lower. Always obey speed limit signs. Some highways are **toll roads**, which means you must pay to use the road.

In smaller cities and towns, Americans usually are careful to obey traffic signs and regulations. They often stop or slow down to let other cars in and out of the traffic pattern. Be very careful at pedestrian crossings. If you see a person trying to cross at a crosswalk, you must stop.

If you do not have your own car, you can rent a car. There are many car rental agencies, and some are cheaper than others. Use the telephone to call and ask for rates, which can be per day or per mile or both. You pay for gas. Remember (section 1.2), you must have a credit card and, of course, a driver's license. If you are a tourist, you may use your own national driver's license.

In most cities you can get around on foot, or by bus, taxi, car, or subway (in large cities). Because of the heavy traffic and limited parking, a car is not always useful in a large city. If you do bring your car to a city, you can park on the street at designated places. These parking spaces usually have **parking meters**, which require coins. Read the instructions carefully, and do not let the meter expire. The police check carefully and, if the meter shows a little red "expired" flag, you will get a parking ticket, which can be very expensive — $25.00 in some large cities. A better place to park is a parking garage. It is more expensive, but it is safer and you don't need to come back to put more money in the meter. Wherever you park in a large city, lock the car and keep packages out of sight. Car stealing is a big problem in cities.

Every city and town has its own public transportation system, and each system is a little different. One thing you should know is that buses often require exact change. (You can ask someone who is waiting at a bus stop.) Taxi (cab) drivers also carry very little change, so have small bills with you when you get in. The taxi drivers expect a tip (see section 1.12).

In smaller towns and rural areas, public transportation is not very good. Most people depend on cars. In warm weather, a bicycle can be a good way to get around town.

You may think about hitchhiking, standing by the roadside and holding out your arm and pointing down the road with your thumb. It is the least expensive and most dangerous way to travel. We do not advise you to do this.

1.9 Shopping

Most businesses and offices in the United States are open from 9:00 A.M. to 5:00 P.M., Monday through Friday. Employees take an hour-long lunch break sometime between noon and 2:00 P.M., but they take breaks at different times so there is always someone to help customers.

Retail stores operate on a slightly different schedule. Most stores in the city center open between 9:00 and 10:00 A.M. and close at 5:30 or 6:00 P.M., except on Fridays, when they often stay open later. They are open on Saturday and during lunch hours.

Outside the city center you will find other shopping areas called **shopping centers** and **malls**. You usually need a car to get there, but parking is free. Malls are covered shopping areas with many different stores and restaurants all under one roof. They are heated and air-conditioned and generally safe. They also stay open until 9:00 P.M., and they are usually open on Sunday.

 **Grocery stores** and **supermarkets** are usually open from 8:00 A.M. until late in the evening. In most towns and cities there will be at least one that is open all day and night, seven days a week.

To help you in your shopping, here is a description of the different kinds of stores you will find in the United States:

Specialty Shops: These are small stores which carry only one or two kinds of merchandise, such as shoes, clothing, books, stationery, antiques, jewelry, hardware, etc.

Chain Stores: These stores operate throughout the country and carry clothing, household goods and appliances, hardware, and furniture at reasonable prices. Some well-known chain stores are JC Penney and Sears. There are also discount chain stores. Some well-known ones are WalMart, K-mart, Ames, Target, Home Depot, and Staples.

Department Stores: These stores are very large and have a wide variety of products. The products are organized into different departments, such as men's, women's, and children's clothing, housewares, furniture, appliances, fabric, toys, etc.

Factory Outlets: These retail stores are run by the manufacturers. They sell their own products at lower prices than those

19

charged by other retail stores. These outlets are often located outside of the city center.

Convenience Stores: These small stores are open all day and late into the evening. They sell basic food items, tobacco, newspapers, and other small items. Their prices are usually higher than those at supermarkets, but they are often close to your home and open when you need them.

Gas Stations: Gas, oil, and other supplies for cars are easily available in the suburbs, in small towns, and along highways. There are few gas stations in the centers of big cities. Nowadays, most stations are self-service. This means you must pump your own gas. In some places, you pay first, then pump. In other places, you pump first and pay after. A sign will tell you what to do. Some stations have full-service pumps. This means an attendant will pump your gas. The attendant may also check your oil and clean your window, if you ask. The attendant does not expect to be tipped.

Some gas stations sell tires and do tire repair, but not all. A few stations have a mechanic to do engine repairs. The Yellow Pages always list local sources for auto care. Auto clubs like **AAA** (American Automobile Association, known as "Triple A") provide maps and travel advice as well as emergency service, towing, and mechanical help to members. Inside many gas stations, there is a small convenience store. Most towns have at least one 24-hour gas station.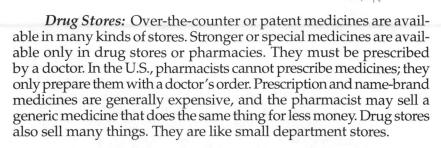

Drug Stores: Over-the-counter or patent medicines are available in many kinds of stores. Stronger or special medicines are available only in drug stores or pharmacies. They must be prescribed by a doctor. In the U.S., pharmacists cannot prescribe medicines; they only prepare them with a doctor's order. Prescription and name-brand medicines are generally expensive, and the pharmacist may sell a generic medicine that does the same thing for less money. Drug stores also sell many things. They are like small department stores.

There are federal taxes on some items purchased in stores in the United States, and most states (and some cities) have a sales tax of 2% to 10%. In many states there is also a room and meals tax on hotel and restaurant bills.

1.10 Health, Medical Care, and Safety

Medical care in the United States is good, but it is also expensive. It is therefore a good idea to purchase health insurance to cover medical expenses in case you have an accident or get sick. For information, write to American International Underwriters, Inc., Investors' Building, Washington, DC 20036.

If you need medical care while traveling, you can call any hospital. Some hospitals have outpatient clinics, or they may help you in the emergency room. The hospital also may give you the name and telephone number of a doctor or a private clinic. There are not many government-supported hospitals in the United States. Most hospitals are private, nonprofit organizations, and their fees are very high.

Water is safe to drink in all American towns and cities.

It is unfortunate but necessary to say that visitors need to be careful about their personal safety, especially in large cities. If you are not familiar with a place, do not explore it alone, especially at night and on foot. First, ask somebody (hosts, hotel personnel, police) for advice on where to go and where NOT to go. While driving, keep car doors locked and windows closed, and do not get out of the car or open the window if you are stopped by someone other than the police. Do not open hotel doors unless you know who is outside. Do not show cash openly.

1.11 Electricity and Electronics

The current in electric outlets in the United States is 110–115 volts, 60-cycle AC rather than the 200–220 volts, 50-cycle AC found in many other countries. Only special outlets for larger machines such as clothes dryers are 200–220 volts. Smaller appliances such as razors, hair dryers, and curlers will work on the lower current. For other appliances, you may need a transformer to change the current to a higher voltage. All plugs in the United States are flat-pronged rather than round. You can purchase adapters to attach to round plugs so they can be used in a flat-pronged outlet.

Videotape systems in the United States may not be the same as in your country. The United States uses only the VHS format with NTSC system. Very few American video players can play PAL/SECAM cassettes. Video stores also carry DVD's (Digital video disks). They can only be used with a DVD palyer.

1.12 Tipping

In restaurants, the usual tip for waiters is 15% (see section 1.3). In most fast food restaurants, you do not tip. In hotels and motels, you leave a tip for the maid only if you stay several days. You should tip 10%–15% for hotel room service people and $1.00 per bag for bellhops. Barbers and hairdressers are usually tipped about 10%–15%, and taxi drivers also expect 10%–15%.

Before tipping roomservice people and waiters, look at your bill to be sure that a service charge has not been included. When you pay by credit card for many services, you will find a place to add a tip to the credit card slip. Some people prefer to pay tips in cash so the specific person they are tipping gets the money.

The following people are not usually tipped in the United States: theater ushers, hotel desk clerks, guides at historical sites, mail carriers, grocery store employees, gas station attendants, and elevator operators.

1.13 Measures

The United States has not adopted the metric system. The following charts will help you to understand and convert to U.S. measurements.

Linear Measurements

U.S.	Metric
1 inch	2.54 centimeters
1 foot	0.3048 meter
1 yard	0.9144 meter
1 mile	1.609 kilometers

Metric	U.S.
1 centimeter	0.39 inch
1 meter	3.28 feet/1.094 yards
1 kilometer	0.62 mile

Liquid Measurements

U.S.	Metric
1 teaspoon (tsp)	5 milliliters
1 tablespoon (tbsp)	15 milliliters
1 cup (c)	0.237 liter
1 pint (pt)	0.473 liter
1 quart (qt)	0.946 liter
1 gallon (gal)	3.785 liters

Metric	U.S.
1 liter	2.1 pints/1.05 quarts

Dry Measurements

U.S.	Metric
1 pint	0.551 liter
1 quart	1.1 liters
1 peck	8.81 liters
1 bushel	35.24 liters

Weights

U.S.	Metric
1 ounce	28.4 grams
1 pound	454 grams
1 ton	0.907 ton

Metric	U.S.
1 gram	0.035 ounce
1 kilogram (kilo)	2.2 pounds
1 ton	1.1 tons

Formulas for Approximate Conversions

1. Yards to meters, multiply by 0.9.
   Meters to yards, multiply by 1.1.

2. Miles to kilometers, multiply by 1.6.
   Kilometers to miles, multiply by 0.6.

3. 1 quart is about 1 liter.
   1 gallon is about 4 liters.

4. 1 pound is about 0.45 kilos.
   1 kilo is about 2.2 pounds.

Temperature

Fahrenheit	Centigrade
100°F	37.8°C
90°F	32.2°C
80°F	26.7°C
70°F	21.1°C
60°F	15.6°C
50°F	10.0°C
40°F	4.4°C
32°F	0°C
10°F	–12°C
0°F	–17.8°C
–10°F	–23°C

Centigrade	Fahrenheit
100°C	212°F
40°C	104°F
30°C	86°F
20°C	68°F
10°C	50°F
0°C	32°F
–10°C	14°F
–20°C	–4°F

The Fahrenheit temperature is approximately twice the Centigrade plus 30:

$$C° \times 2 + 30 = approx. F°$$

$$F° - 30)/2 = approx. C°$$

Clothing Sizes

Women		Men	
Skirts, dresses, coats		Coats, jackets	
U.S.	Europe	U.S.	Europe
10	38	36	46
12	40	38	48
14	42	40	50
16	44	42	54
18	46	44	56
20	48	46	59

Blouses, sweaters		Shirts	
30	38	14	36
32	40	$14^1/_2$	37
34	42	15	38
36	44	$15^1/_2$	39
38	46	16	40
40	48	$16^1/_2$	41
		17	42

Shoes		Shoes	
5	35	8	41
$5^1/_2$	35	$8^1/_2$	42
6	36	$9 - 9^1/_2$	43
7	38	$10 - 10^1/_2$	44
8	$38^1/_2$	$11 - 11^1/_2$	45
$8^1/_2$	39	$12 - 12^1/_2$	46
9	40	13	47

2. Customs and Values

The topics in this section will help you begin your study of American culture — the way Americans think and believe and act. We will make generalizations that may not be true for the people you meet, live, or study with. One generalization which you should always remember is that there is great variety among the states of America and the people of America. It is a culture formed from many cultures.

2.1 Greetings and Leave-takings

Americans do not spend time over long greetings. **"Hello"** or **"Hi, how are you?"** or **"How are you doing?"** is often sufficient.

When meeting someone for the first time, Americans usually shake hands. Young people may not shake hands, while older people, particularly men, continue the tradition. Very often, Americans neglect to introduce new people to one another. This is not a problem, as most people are comfortable introducing themselves if no introduction occurs. You should give your name when someone introduces himself or herself to you. If you don't, they will then ask your name. When someone older is introduced in America, she or he will usually respond with **"How do you do?"** or **"Nice to meet you."** This is not true for young Americans, who may only respond to an introduction with **"Hi."**

Leave-takings are often as brief as greetings. **"'Bye"** or **"See you later"** usually is enough. It is also common for people to take leave of one another by saying, **"We should get together sometime,"** or **"You should come over sometime,"** or **"I'll call you soon."** Don't be disappointed if someone says, "I'll call you," and never does, or suggests that you come over sometime and never invites you. These are all formulas for farewells; they do not necessarily mean that the individual will actually do what she or he has suggested.

2.2 Names and Titles

Titles based on social class are not used in the United States. Some titles based on occupation, such as **Ambassador, Senator, Governor, Father,** and **Rabbi** are used. Occupations usually carrying titles are: diplomats, clergy, court judges, military officers, medical and academic doctors, and government officials. Individuals in other occupations are usually referred to with **Mr.** ("mister") and **Ms.** (pronounced "mizz") followed by the last or family name. You will hear the older titles **Miss** for unmarried women and **Mrs.** ("missiz") for married women, but most professional women prefer Ms.

Many Americans, however, do not want to use titles and family names in conversation. Even if someone is introduced to you with a title, don't be surprised if they tell you to call them by their first name. If you insist on calling individuals by their titles when they have asked you not to, you will be perceived as being more formal than necessary. However, young people are often expected to call older people, such as the parents of their friends, by their last name preceded by Mr., Ms., Miss, or Mrs., or a title. This is the polite form of address in this situation, and you should follow it if you are younger than the person to whom you are talking. If they want you to call them by their first name, they will say so. Otherwise, if you use their first name, they may think you are being impolite.

2.3 Conversation Topics

Americans often ask a lot of questions when they first meet someone, and some of these questions may seem quite personal to you. When an American does this, she or he is only looking for a common ground for building a relationship. Perhaps you will discover similar interests or abilities which can then be used as a basis for friendship.

Although Americans ask a lot of questions, there are some topics that you should avoid in conversation until you know a person well: the person's age and financial status, the cost of the person's clothes or personal belongings, his or her personal religious beliefs, and a person's love (or sex) life.

2.4 Friendship

Americans are open and friendly to newcomers. Perhaps this is because they are very mobile, and they have learned to make new friends quickly. This easy friendliness does not mean, however, that they will try to develop a long and deep friendship with you. This kind of relationship takes time in the United States, as it does anywhere. Remember, Americans often move their homes from one town to another, so it is not easy for them to develop long-lasting friendships.

2.5 Invitations

Americans will quickly and easily invite strangers into their homes. You will find that you are treated as "one of the family" almost immediately after you arrive. Do not be surprised at American informality. It is quite natural. Your hosts will probably not give you very special guest status. You should "make yourself at home" with them. If you are invited to a home for a meal or a party, you can ask, **"Can I bring anything?"** If you are invited for a stay of one night or more, then it is appropriate to bring a small gift — flowers, candy, or some souvenir from your own country.

If you receive a written invitation, it is important to respond to it as soon as possible. Some invitations will have **R.S.V.P.** or "Please reply" written at the bottom, and these must have a reply. If a telephone number is given, then it is polite to call and accept or decline the invitation. If there is no phone number, then a written note is adequate. If you receive an invitation over the telephone, make sure that you have correctly understood the date, time, and location. And if for some reason you should realize later that you cannot attend, then be sure to telephone to inform the person inviting you that you will not be there, and explain the reason why.

2.6 Personal Space and Privacy

These notes on personal space are very general. Customs vary in different parts of the country and between ethnic groups. However, in general, Americans don't touch each other very much in public. Touching between two people of the same sex is not common. (Touching between two men is sometimes considered a sign of homosexuality.) Touching between people of different sex is more common, especially if they are young lovers. You may see young men and women holding hands, embracing, and even kissing in public. In the past, this kind of open touching was considered very impolite. But times are changing, and nowadays people are more likely to touch and show affection in public. In fact, it isn't unusual to hug someone if you have not seen them in a long time, or if they or you are going away.

In conversations, Americans stand about 2 to 3 feet apart and often use a lot of gestures. Some gestures involve physical contact. Sympathy is shown by putting a hand on another person's shoulder. Touching the other person's hand or arm shows support, agreement, or thanks.

Americans are not especially private people. They leave the doors to their offices open, and often neighboring homes are not separated by fences or walls. It is also rare to find closed doors in homes.

2.7 Time

Being on time is important in the United States. A few guidelines are given here.

When you are invited for a meal, you should arrive within 5 to 15 minutes of the time specified in the invitation. Do not arrive earlier, because people usually do their own cooking, and they may be working until the last minute to get things ready for you. If you are going to be late, it is polite to call and inform the people who have invited you. Then they can prepare the meal according to the time you will actually arrive.

When you are invited to a party or dance, you can arrive up to half an hour "late." For cocktail parties and receptions, a time period is usually specified during which you are expected to arrive and leave. You may arrive at any time during that period, but remember that you are also expected to leave by the ending time indicated.

For movies and theater productions, you will want to arrive at least 10 minutes ahead of time to get your ticket/program and be seated. You should also be at least 10 minutes early for weddings, funerals, lectures, and sports events.

For business appointments, you should arrive exactly on time or a few minutes before your appointment. If the person you are seeing is busy, she or he may keep you waiting, but you should still be on time.

2.8 Silence

Many Americans are uncomfortable with silence when they are with another person. When there is silence in a conversation, they may start talking to stop the silence. Students often study with music playing in the background, and people working around the house will often have the television or radio on "to keep them company." If you are silent in a conversation or a gathering for a long time, Americans will try to "draw you out" (get you to talk) and may even ask if you are all right or if there is anything they can do to help you. One important note: Americans may remain silent when you say something they don't agree with because they feel uncomfortable disagreeing with someone they don't know well.

2.9 Equality

The concept of **equality** is extremely important in the United States. Americans generally say that all people are the same, regardless of social, economic, racial, ethnic, or gender differences. They expect to have an equal opportunity to achieve personal and professional goals. Americans can become very angry if they think they are not being given an equal opportunity to compete or improve their lives. Fair government and equal protection by law are very important. Americans may also become angry at people who expect special favors or treatment. When they think someone is not being fair or is looking for special treatment, they are likely to say, "Who do you think you are?" They also get angry at people who will not wait for their turn.

There are, of course, social and class differences in the United States and many inequalities in American life. Most Americans are aware of these inequalities, but they would rather think that the United States is a country where, to quote the Declaration of Independence, "all men are created equal" and have certain rights, and "among these are Life, Liberty and the pursuit of Happiness."

Partly because of this strong belief in equality, Americans may seem very informal. But informality does not mean a lack of respect. It shows individual equality — an important American value.

2.10 Independence

Americans value personal independence and self-reliance. This individualistic orientation means that people believe they are responsible for their own happiness and future, and that they should not depend on others to make them happy and successful. This does not mean that they do not work together or help one another or cooperate. It means that each person is responsible for his or her own life.

This individualism is seen in many ways in American life. For example, the great American hero, the mythical cowboy, is a strong, independent individual. The emphasis on individualism begins early. Children are encouraged to develop and express their own opinions and interests, particularly in school. In family life, children are often given household responsibilities at an early age. Teenagers are expected to find summer jobs when they are not in school. And American young people often leave home early to live "on their own."

2.11 Eating Customs

Americans eat with a knife and fork in the following way: When cutting, they hold the knife in the right hand and the fork in the left. After cutting, the knife is placed on the edge of the plate and the fork is shifted to the right hand for eating. While eating, the left hand is often placed on the lap. Left-handed people eat with their left hand.

Here are some other rules to follow when eating with Americans.

- Keep your mouth closed when you are chewing food, and speak only when your mouth is empty.
- When you need something that is not near you on the table, ask the person closest to the item to pass it to you; do not reach across in front of them to get it yourself.
- If someone offers you more to eat and you would like to have more, accept their offer. They will not repeat the offer or insist that you eat. If you don't want more, they will accept your refusal.
- Do not burp after eating.
- Try not to rest your arms on the table while you are eating.
- If you need to leave the table while others are still eating, ask, "Would you excuse me, please?"

Most Americans eat three times a day, and may also have a snack and coffee mid-morning and mid-afternoon. A complete **breakfast** consists of fruit juice and cereal or eggs. Eggs are usually accompanied by toast and bacon or sausage. Adults drink coffee or tea and children drink milk. Special breakfast dishes served less frequently (typically on weekends and holidays) include waffles, French toast, and pancakes, served with butter and maple syrup.

Lunch is usually eaten during an hour between noon and 2:00 P.M. People at work and school rarely go home for lunch; they bring a lunch with them in a paper bag or lunch box, or buy something. A typical lunch might consist of one or two sandwiches (see section 1.2), a piece of fruit, and sometimes a small bag of chips (potato or corn chips are popular) and/or a few cookies. Many people working in offices will eat at nearby restaurants.

Dinner is the main meal in the United States. It is eaten in the evening, usually after 6:00 P.M. It usually consists of a meat, fish, or poultry dish with cooked vegetables and a starch such as rice or potatoes. Dessert is common in many homes.

In some families a late evening **snack** may be common. Salty or sweet snacks may be eaten while watching television or just before going to bed.

2.12 Family Life

It is difficult to generalize about how families live in America. There is a great variety of economic, cultural, and regional lifestyles. However, a few observations can be made.

Typically, the family unit which lives together consists of parents and children only. Older people do not generally live with their children who have families of their own. They do, however, keep in touch with their children and remain interested in the well-being of their grandchildren. Typical families have one or two parents and one to three children. Divorce and unwed pregnancy have made the single parent family much more common than it was in the past.

You will find that Americans often have a family pet — usually a dog or cat. The pet is like one of the family and lives in the house with the people. Americans often talk to their pets and spend a lot of money on them.

Children are expected to leave their parents' home when they become adults. Parents and their children often live far away from one another. Usually job opportunities are responsible for the separation of family members, but the family keeps in touch by mail, phone, or e-mail and will travel to help one another in times of difficulty or to share holiday celebrations.

Americans expect their children to choose their own careers and their own spouses. This is again part of the individualism Americans value so highly (see section 2.10).

Within the society as well as within the family, differences between male and female roles are decreasing. The women's movement has helped make people aware that, in the past, women had fewer opportunities than men to pursue personal and professional interests because of the great demand put upon them to remain at home and care for their children. This is changing, and many more women are working outside the home. In many families, the man is assuming more responsibility for child rearing in order to allow the woman to develop a professional career.

In general, men still do not do very much housework. Children, on the other hand, are often given tasks to do on a regular basis, such as setting the table for dinner, watering the garden, folding the laundry, etc. For this work they are often given a sum of money as a weekly allowance. This allowance gives them some responsibility for paying for their personal expenses, such as snacks and tickets to the movies.

Older people are not given the same degree of respect they receive in many other countries. Because they do not usually live with their children, they live on their own as long as they are able to take care of themselves. Then they may live in special homes for the aged where their children and grandchildren can come to visit them. However, the status of older people may be changing. People are living longer because of improved medical care, and they are becoming politically organized and working to ensure that they will be respected and valued. In many stores and businesses, discounts are now given to senior citizens. Many communities provide senior citizen centers where older people can meet and socialize.

2.13 Leisure

Sports of all types are popular in the United States, and facilities for playing various sports exist in all cities and towns: swimming pools, tennis courts, football and baseball fields, golf courses, bowling alleys, skating rinks, skateboard parks, etc. In addition, many Americans have taken up jogging and bicycling in order to stay physically fit. You will probably see joggers almost anywhere you go.

Other popular sports are skiing (on water in warm weather and on snow in the winter), sailing, fishing, hiking, and camping. There are also exercise groups and fitness clubs in most communities. These are groups that do physical exercises to music and centers where exercise equipment is available.

Television is a part of everyday life. Most American families have at least one television and watch it regularly. On weekends, going to the movies is a popular pastime, as is going out for a meal at a restaurant. In warm weather, Americans enjoy picnics and barbecues where food is cooked and eaten outside and people play outdoor games.

Most houses now have one or more computers. They are used for exploring (surfing) the internet for information and for on-line shopping. Video games are very popular, and many people spend a lot of time playing games on their computers.

Americans also like to read, do various crafts, watch sports events, and attend concerts. They also enjoy gardening and "do-it-yourself" projects, such as sewing their own clothes or building furniture, as might be expected where independence is valued.

2.14 Holidays

Although there may be some local differences, there are ten national holidays. On a national holiday, schools, banks, government offices, and many businesses are closed. The exact date for five of the holidays changes from year to year because these holidays are celebrated on Mondays so people can have a long weekend. Here is a list of national holidays.

New Year's Day — January 1
Martin Luther King's Birthday — Third Monday in January
Presidents' Day — Third Monday in February
Memorial Day — Last Monday in May
Independence Day — July 4
Labor Day — First Monday in September
Columbus Day — Second Monday in October
Veterans' Day — November 11
Thanksgiving — Fourth Thursday in November
Christmas — December 25

Some special holiday celebrations and traditions are described below.

Valentine's Day: On February 14, people give cards, flowers, and candy to each other to celebrate love.

Easter: Celebrated in March or April, Easter Sunday is a religious holiday commemorating Jesus Christ's rise from the dead. Many of its traditions, however, are pagan in origin and are observed in American families even when the religious significance is not. On the night before Easter, an imaginary creature known as the Easter Bunny comes to visit children and leaves a basket filled with candy in the shape of eggs, bunnies, and baby chicks. Another tradition is dyeing hard-boiled eggs different colors and painting designs on them. It is common to hide these eggs, as well as candy eggs, for children to look for on Easter Sunday. This is called an Easter egg hunt.

Independence Day: July 4, 1776, was when the thirteen American colonies declared independence from England. "The Fourth" is usually celebrated by parades and picnics with friends and family, followed by fireworks displays in the evening.

Thanksgiving: The first Thanksgiving was celebrated by the early Pilgrim settlers in Massachusetts in 1621, in gratitude for their first successful harvest. They experienced difficulty in those early times and survived only with the help of Native Americans who taught them how to grow and harvest such foods as squash

38

and corn. The Pilgrims' Thanksgiving lasted three days and was celebrated with their Native American friends. Today, Thanksgiving is a four-day holiday for most Americans, many of whom travel home for a family celebration. The major meal is served on Thursday and usually includes certain traditional dishes: roast turkey, potatoes and yams, cranberry sauce, vegetables, and pumpkin and/or mincemeat pie for dessert.

Halloween: Halloween is celebrated on October 31st and, like Easter, includes pagan customs although its name has religious origins. The name is a shortened version of All Hallows Eve, the night before All Saints' Day, which is celebrated by some religious groups on November 1st.

Halloween is customarily celebrated by children who dress up in costumes and go "trick-or-treating." Wearing their costumes, they go to various homes and offer adults an alternative: a "trick" (some mischief they will do to the adult) or a "treat" such as candy (which the adult can give to keep the children from doing mischief). The threat of a trick is not taken seriously today. Halloween is a favorite holiday with children and is often celebrated in school.

Christmas, Hanukkah, and Kwanza: These holidays are celebrated in December. Christmas is celebrated on December 25th to commemorate the birth of Jesus Christ. There are many customs associated with this holiday: exchanging gifts; Santa Claus, who leaves toys for children under the Christmas tree the night before Christmas; decorating the home with evergreens; singing Christmas carols; and sending Christmas cards to friends and acquaintances. Christmas is officially a national holiday and is celebrated in some way by many non-Christians as well as Christians.

Hanukkah is the Jewish Festival of Lights, a celebration of religious freedom. The actual date depends on the Jewish calendar, but it is always celebrated in December and lasts for eight days. Beginning on December 26th, Kwanza is a seven-day holiday based on an African harvest festival; it celebrates the diversity of cultures and religions in Africa and around the world. As with Hanukkah, traditional wisdom is shared with children as ceremonial candles are lit each day.

New Year's Eve: New Year's Eve is celebrated on December 31st with parties that last beyond midnight so that everyone can celebrate the first minutes of the New Year. In many places the celebrations are called "First Night." January 1st is always a holiday, and New Year's Day is celebrated with parades in some cities.

2.15 The Environment

In recent years Americans have become more and more conscious of the natural environment and the problems of pollution. For that reason, waste disposal is important. Do not throw litter (paper, cans, bottles) on the roadside or in parks or even in the forest. Many Americans become very angry when they see someone littering, and in some places there is a heavy fine for littering.

In many places it is important to separate and recycle (use again) certain plastic, glass, and aluminum containers. In some places this material is picked up by the town or city waste disposal truck. In other places you must take it to a recycling center.

2.16 Business Etiquette

In the business world, it is customary for men to wear a tie with a business suit or, in a less formal office, a tie with a sports jacket and slacks. Women wear a business suit or a dress. A suit with dress pants is less formal. Until you know the office, it is best to be formal.

It is very important to be on time for business meetings and appointments. Always try to arrive at least five minutes before the scheduled time. If you must be late, telephone ahead to say that you will not be on time, and, when you arrive, always apologize and give an explanation for being late. When you first arrive at the office, it is a good idea to ask the receptionist how much time you have. Then you will have an idea about when the meeting will end.

The American businessperson will probably greet you with a handshake, a smile, and an offer of coffee or tea. It is not necessary to accept the offer. You should expect that smoking will not be allowed. It is a good idea to offer your business card at this time, especially if your name is a little difficult for an American to say.

The first few minutes of the conversation will probably be "small talk" about the weather, your trip, your impressions of America or the city you are in. Let the American host shift the conversation to business. You should look at the person you are talking with, but look away frequently; do not stare, and do not wear sunglasses. It is important to be direct, but it is not good to be very direct or aggressive, nor is it good to be very vague or indecisive. If you have a colleague and you talk to each other in your native language, tell your American host what you are talking about.

At first, you should address people as "Mr." or "Ms.," but after a few minutes the American may begin to call you by your first name. This is fairly common, and it is O.K. for you to do the same.

When you think the meeting is coming to an end, you should take a minute to be sure that you understand what the next step will be. When the meeting ends, you will be expected to shake hands again.

In some cases you may be invited to lunch, You will not be expected to pay for the lunch or even to share the bill. If you invite an American to lunch, however, you should pay. They may try to pay or share the bill, and if they are very insistent you can suggest that they pay for the taxi or leave the tip. When an American offers to share the bill, it is not because they think you are poor, but rather because in America, people like to think that the best relationships are those based on an equal footing.

3. Country Facts

As you become more comfortable living in the United States, you may want to know more facts about the country — for example, how it is organized and governed. This section includes information about the history, people, and institutions of the United States.

3.1 History

The first inhabitants of North, South, and Central America came about 50,000 years ago from Asia. The first Europeans to come were probably the Vikings, who arrived about 1000 A.D. from Greenland but did not establish permanent settlements.

Christopher Columbus is credited with "discovering" America in 1492. This "discovery" caused much excitement in Europe, and explorers from several countries began exploring various parts of the "new" continents during the 1500s. The Spanish and Portuguese explored the Southern Hemisphere. The Spanish conquered the powerful empires of the Incas in Peru and the Aztecs in Mexico. Then they started settlements in what is now the western United States as far north as northern California. Later the British, Dutch, and French explored the east coast of North America, establishing permanent settlements there. The French settlements became eastern Canada; the British and Dutch settlements became the United States.

By the 1700s, there were thirteen British colonies along the east coast of what is now the United States. They stretched from New Hampshire in the north to Georgia in the south. Each colony had a legislature made up of colonists but was under the control of Britain.

Economic opportunity and religious and political freedom attracted increasing numbers of settlers to the British colonies. Most came from Britain, but people from almost every other western European country also came. The colonists rejected the idea that government was something inherited from the past. They regarded it as something they themselves should design and control and, although they lived under British rule, they often did not follow British laws.

Relations between the American colonies and Britain became worse during the 1700s. The British tried to tighten control over the colonies by passing laws that restricted freedoms and increased taxes, but the Americans had been governing themselves and had developed their own sense of self-government. Controls from Britain were resented, and this resentment eventually developed into conflict in 1775. The Revolutionary War began, and on July 4,1776, the colonists declared independence from England. In 1783 the British were finally defeated and forced to accept American independence.

The United States of America was officially formed in 1776 with the adoption of the **Declaration of Independence**. This set forth certain "truths" that the writers felt were self-evident: that all men are created equal and are endowed by their Creator with rights to life, liberty, and the pursuit of happiness. Governments were formed to protect those rights and should therefore derive their powers with the consent of the people they govern. A new government was set up under laws called the **Articles of Confederation** (1781), which were replaced by the **U.S. Constitution** in 1788. This outlined the basic form of government for the nation and is still the basis for American government today (see section 3.4).

The main political and social issue causing disagreement among the American states in the 1800s was **slavery**. Slaves were the main work force for the plantation system of farming used in the South. Slavery was first outlawed in the northern states, but the southern states continued the tradition because it provided cheap labor. The southern states tried to secede from the Union but were told by the North that the United States must be preserved. So in 1861 the **Civil War** broke out between the North and the South. This was the most tragic period of United States history; thousands of lives were lost and large parts of the South were left in ruins. The North won the war in 1865, and slavery was outlawed throughout the country soon thereafter.

Throughout the 1800s, settlers moved farther and farther west, and by 1890 settlements had been established all across the country to the Pacific coast. The settlement of the West brought disaster to many of the Native American tribes. The Natives had no chance against the superior weapons of the settlers, and those who fought back were killed or forced to live in certain areas called reservations. By 1900 the Native American way of life had become almost a thing of the past.

Rapid industrial growth occurred from 1870 to 1916. The value of goods produced during this period increased ten times, and the country grew in many ways as a result. In 1917, the United States entered into **World War I** in Europe and played an important role until the war ended on November 11, 1918. From then until 1929, the United States experienced great economic growth. Investors invested more and more money. But the economy was not strong; only part of it was growing — manufacturing. And so in 1929 the stock market collapsed and the Great Depression began. During this period, millions of workers lost their jobs and poverty became a serious problem.

Not only the American economy was depressed. Many other countries had the same problems, and as a result, certain leaders gained power in Germany, Italy and Japan with promises of changing the economic situation. Adolf Hitler in Germany and a group of military leaders in Japan began conquering neighbor-ing countries, and their actions led to **World War II**. From 1941 to 1945, the United States fought and with its allies won this war. First, Nazi Germany was defeated, caught between the USSR on the east and the US and Great Britain, with help from the free French, Canadians, and several other allies on the West. The Allies then turned to defeat the Japanese by pushing them off the mainland of Asia and off island after island moving closer to the home islands of Japan itself. Rather than invade Japan causing a terrible loss of life both among the allied troops and among the Japanese, President Harry Truman made the decision to try the new, secret weapon the United States had been developing, the atomic bomb. After a second bomb was dropped, the Japanese surrendered.

Following World War II, under the leadership of President Truman and George Marshall, who had been the head of the allied war effort and was now Secretary of State, the United States tried a new experiment. For the first time in history, the winner of a war rebuilt the nations it had defeated. New democratic governments were started by the Germans and the Japanese, governments that accepted many of the ideals and the civil rights of the American system. Then under the Marshall Plan, the American goverment rebuilt the economies of the defeated nations. This brought on a long period of general peace and prosperity.

The United States began its greatest period of economic growth. Roads were built opening the whole country to truck and automobile traffic. New industries grew quickly driven by the growing consumer economy. From 1948 to the present America became richer and more powerful as its trade boomed within the United States and internationally. Most Americans have faith in the system and "the American Dream." This is the idea that in America you are free to work hard and save and invest your money so you can live a good life and maybe get rich; if you are educated and smart and work very hard, you may get very rich, and you have a right to do so.

However, America is never simple. As the country became richer and more powerful, there were problems. Internationally, the US and its new allies, NATO, including Germany, Great Britain, France, and Canada, and Japan, fought the long Cold War with the Soviet Union and other communist countries. Winston Churchill, the British Prime Minister, said that an "Iron Curtain" came down dividing Europe, and he spoke of the "balance of terror" that kept the major powers from going to war, immobilized for fear of the atom and then hydrogen bombs that the Americans and Russians developed. Eventually, the cost of this Cold War with its arms race became so great that the Soviet system collapsed, freeing its subject nations, and the war ended in the late 1980's.

The cost of the Cold War was very great. The stockpiles of weapons that could kill everything on Earth, even if they were used by mistake, cost both sides money that should have been used in productive ways. Both sides became involved in terrible hot wars that cost too much money, too many lives, and deep disillusionment among the people. The first was the Korean War between South Korea, aided by the United Nations forces led by the U.S., and North Korea, aided by Russia's newly communist ally, "Red" China. After three years of suffering (1950-1953), the war ended with no gain of land on either side. Then came the long war in Vietnam and the rest of Southeast Asia that poisoned the land and the lives of most of the people who fought and those who just lived through it. The United States left without winning, and the North Vietnamese eventually took over the South. But no one really won. The people of the region were left an impoverished and brutalized world. Then America and the U.N. watched as a communist/nationalist government in Cambodia killed millions of its people. Finally, the U.S.S.R. in an attempt to gain control of its neighboring Islamic country, Afghanistan, took one side in another civil war. The Russians finally withdrew without winning

45

and with losses that contributed to the collapse of the Soviet government. America had survived the Cold War as the world's strongest military and economic "superpower." But there were costs.

Internally, the United States was strong, but many different groups of citizens were dissatisfied in many different ways. In the 1950's, young people began to rebell against "the system," a movement which through many changes has continued to the present. They demanded freedom and social change but often ended up with drugs, alcohol, and sex. Many other Americans, dissatisfied by the commercialism of their society, turned to religions of many different and sometimes strange kinds. Prosperity pleased the majority of Americans, but many minority groups remained poor. American history since World War II has been characterized by continuous social change brought about through public protest on various issues in American life. Some major movements have been: the civil rights movement, aimed at gaining equality for African Americans; protests against American involvement in the Vietnam War; the  women's liberation movement; the gay rights movement (for equal rights for homosexuals); various movements against both military and industrial uses of nuclear power; and, most recently, a growing awareness of the pollution and destruction of the environment.

Although the growth of trade worldwide during the last fifty years has brought greater prosperity to many people, many other people around the world have been dissatisfied. The United States and the other leading industrial nations have not solved the problems of increasing population and poverty, the ever growing "gap" between rich and poor individuals and nations, environmental degradation, racist and sexist injustice, and what some people see as cultural and spiritual imperialism and corruption. Since the end of the Cold War, these problems have stimulated popular protests in many parts of the world, and these protests have stimulated much positive change. However, in combination with nationalist conflicts all around the world, these protest movements have also stimulated the growth of terrorist organizations. In 2001, this terrorism finally struck the United States with the attacks on the Pentagon and New York's World Trade Towers. Nations around the world began working together in many ways to suppress terrorists.

Four Noteworthy American Presidents

George Washington, 1732–1799

George Washington, who became the first U.S. president, was born in 1732 in Virginia, where his father was a prosperous planter. After serving heroically as commander in chief of the Continental army in the American Revolution, he presided in 1787 over the convention that wrote the constitution. Many leaders contributed to this process, but without Washington's stern and fair moral leadership, it was said, the constitution could not have been written. Washington was unanimously voted the first president in 1789 and was reelected in 1793. Setting the standard of the two-term presidency, he retired in 1798. He died at his home at Mount Vernon in 1799. All over the world today, it is common for national heroes to be called "the George Washington" of their country.

Abraham Lincoln, 1809–1865

Abraham Lincoln, the sixteenth U.S. president, was born in a log cabin to a Kentucky farm family who moved to Indiana when he was still very young. Later, he settled in Illinois, where he studied law on his own and served in the state legislature as a member of the Whig party. He was elected to the U.S. House of Representatives in 1847 and in 1858 ran unsuccessfully for the U.S. Senate against Stephen A. Douglas. The Lincoln–Douglas debates brought Lincoln to public attention for his antislavery positions, and in 1860 he became the presidential nominee of the new

Republican party. His election prompted the Southern states to secede from the Union and form the Confederacy. During the civil war that followed (1861–1865), Lincoln issued the Emancipation Proclamation, which defined the war as a crusade against slavery. His well-known Gettysburg Address (1863) further defined the war as the struggle for preservation of "government of the people, by the people, for the people." In 1865, immediately after the Union victory, Lincoln was assassinated by John Wilkes Booth.

Franklin Delano Roosevelt, 1882–1945

Franklin Delano Roosevelt, the thirty-second U.S. president, was born in Hyde Park, New York, into the same patrician family that had produced his distant cousin President Theodore Roosevelt and his wife, Eleanor Roosevelt. Despite an attack of polio in 1921 that left him unable to walk without assistance, he ran successfully for governor of New York and served from 1929 to 1933. He easily defeated Republican Herbert Hoover in 1932, during the Great Depression, and launched an ambitious economic and social program, the "New Deal," designed to put people to work, get the economy moving, and create hope. Although the Depression did not end until the onset of World War II, Roosevelt's efforts earned him the loyalty of working people; he was re-elected by a landslide vote in 1936 and won third and fourth terms, as well, in 1940 and 1944. Having seen the country through World War II, Roosevelt died of a stroke less than four weeks before the Nazi surrender in 1945. He continues to be regarded as one of the three or four greatest American presidents.

John Fitzgerald Kennedy, 1917–1963

John F. Kennedy, the thirty-fifth U.S. president, was born in Brookline, Massachusetts, of Irish-American descent. Wounded in World War II, he entered politics after the war and was elected as a Democrat to the U.S. House of Representatives (1947–1953) and then the Senate (1953–1961). In 1960 he was elected U.S. president, the first Catholic and, at age 43, the youngest man to win that office. He is remembered for his active support of desegregation, for his "New Frontier" social programs, and for establishing the Peace Corps. In 1962 he brought the country to the brink of nuclear war in the Cuban missile crisis, but the following year he secured a nuclear test ban treaty with the USSR. In November of that year, his presidency was cut short when he was assassinated in Dallas, Texas.

48

Three Noteworthy American Prophets

In 1963, one year before he was awarded the Nobel Peace Prize and five years before he was assassinated at the age of 39, civil rights leader Martin Luther King, Jr., gave a speech to a Peace March at the Lincoln Memorial in Washington, D.C. That speech gave a new, deep meaning to the expression "the American Dream." King was a modern prophet, and in his "I Have a Dream" speech, he referred to the writings of two earlier American prophets, Thomas Jefferson, who wrote the Declaration of Independence and later was the third U.S. president, and Abraham Lincoln.

Thomas Jefferson, from the *Declaration of Independence, 1776*

We hold these Truths to be self-evident, that all Men are created equal, that they are endowed by their Creator with certain inalienable Rights, that among these are Life, Liberty, and the Pursuit of Happiness – That to secure these Rights, Governments are instituted among Men, deriving their just Powers from the Consent of the Governed.

Abraham Lincoln, from the *Gettysburg Address, 1863*

Fourscore and seven years ago our fathers brought forth on this continent a new nation, conceived in liberty and dedicated to the proposition that all men are created equal.

Now we are engaged in a great civil war, testing whether that nation or any nation so conceived and so dedicated, can long endure. We are met on a great battle field of that war. We have come to dedicate a portion of that field as a final resting place for those who here gave their lives that that nation might live. It is altogether fitting and proper that we should do this.

But, in a larger sense, we cannot dedicate – we cannot consecrate – we cannot hallow this ground. The brave men, living and dead, who struggled here, have consecrated it, far above our poor power to add or to detract. The world will little note nor long remember what we say here, but it can never forget what they did here. It is for us the living, rather, to be here dedicated to the great task remaining before us – that from these honored dead we take increased devotion – that we here highly resolve that these dead shall not have died in vain – that this nation, under God, shall have a new birth of freedom – and that government of the people, by the people, for the people, shall not perish from the earth.

Martin Luther King, Jr., from *I Have a Dream*, 1963

Fivescore years ago., a great American, in whose symbolic shadow we stand, signed the Emancipation Proclamation. This momentous decree came as a great beacon of hope to millions of Negro slaves who had been seared in the flames of withering injustice. It came as a joyous daybreak to end the long night of captivity. But one hundred years later, we must face the tragic fact that the Negro is still not free...

I say to you today, my friends, that in spite of difficulties and frustrations of the moment I still have a dream. It is a dream deeply rooted in the American Dream.

I have a dream that one day this nation will rise up and live out the true meaning of its creed: "We hold these truths to be self-evident; that all men are created equal."

I have a dream that one day on the red hills of Georgia the sons of former slaves and the sons of former slave-owners will be able to sit down together at the table of brotherhood.

I have a dream that one day even the state of Mississippi, a desert state sweltering with the heat of injustice and oppression, will be transformed into an oasis of freedom and justice.

I have a dream that my four little children will one day live in a nation where they will not be judged by the color of their skin but by the content of their character....

When we let freedom ring, when we let it ring from every village and every hamlet, from every state and every city, we will be able to speed up that day when all God's children, black men and white men, Jews and Gentiles, Protestants and Catholics, will be able to join hands and sing in the words of the old Negro spiritual, "Free at last! Free at last! Thank God almighty, we are free at last!"

3.2 Political Map

On the next page (page 51) you will find a map of the 50 states. The key to the map is on page 52. Each state is also listed with its postal abbreviation.

Washington, D.C. (District of Columbia) is between the states of Maryland and Virginia. It is a federal district and does not belong to any state.

Puerto Rico and the United States Virgin Islands are not states, but they are associated with the United States, as are the Pacific Islands of Guam (GU), American Samoa (AS), Federated States of Micronesia (FM), Marshall Islands (MH), Northern Mariana Islands (MP), and Palau (PW).

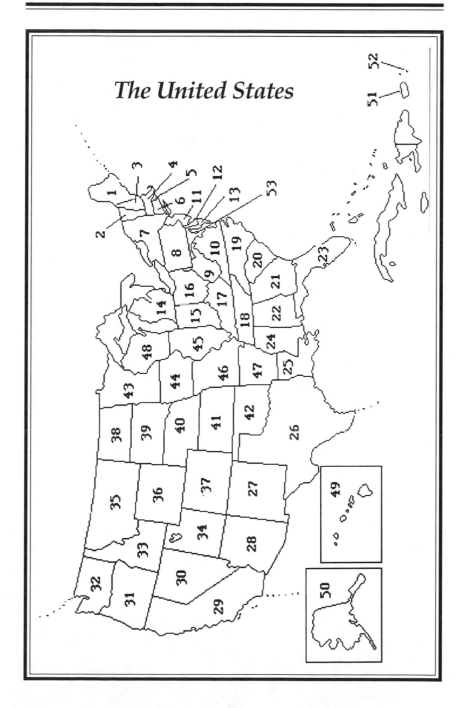

The United States

1	ME	Maine	28	AZ	Arizona
2	VT	Vermont	29	CA	California
3	NH	New Hampshire	30	NV	Nevada
4	MA	Massachusetts	31	OR	Oregon
5	RI	Rhode Island	32	WA	Washington
6	CT	Connecticut	33	ID	Idaho
7	NY	New York	34	UT	Utah
8	PA	Pennsylvania	35	MT	Montana
9	WV	West Virginia	36	WY	Wyoming
10	VA	Virginia	37	CO	Colorado
11	NJ	New Jersey	38	ND	North Dakota
12	DE	Delaware	39	SD	South Dakota
13	MD	Maryland	40	NE	Nebraska
14	MI	Michigan	41	KS	Kansas
15	IN	Indiana	42	OK	Oklahoma
16	OH	Ohio	43	MN	Minnesota
17	KY	Kentucky	44	IA	Iowa
18	TN	Tennessee	45	IL	Illinois
19	NC	North Carolina	46	MO	Missouri
20	SC	South Carolina	47	AR	Arkansas
21	GA	Georgia	48	WI	Wisconsin
22	AL	Alabama	49	HI	Hawaii
23	FL	Florida	50	AK	Alaska
24	MS	Mississippi	51	PR	Puerto Rico
25	LA	Louisiana	52	VI	Virgin Islands
26	TX	Texas	53	DC	District of Columbia
27	NM	New Mexico			

3.3 Land and People

The United States is the fourth largest country in the world in area and the third in population. Its land and climate vary from region to region, and its peoples have come from all of the major cultures of the world.

Regions There are seven regions in the United States, not including Alaska (AK) and Hawaii (Hl). They are listed below. The 48 states listed below are sometimes called the **continental** or **contiguous** (touching) states. In Alaska they are called the "lower 48," and in Hawaii people call them "the mainland."

New England		*Midwest*	
ME	MA	IL	MO
NH	CT	IN	NE
VT	RI	IA	ND
		KS	OH
Mid-Atlantic		MI	SD
NY	DE	MN	WI
NJ	MD		
PA		*Rocky Mountains*	
		CO	NV
South		ID	UT
AL	MS	MT	WY
AR	NC		
FL	SC	*Southwest*	
GA	TN	AZ	OK
KY	VA	NM	TX
LA	WV		
		Pacific or West Coast	
		CA	WA
		OR	

Note: The state names abbreviated in the list above are given with their abbreviations on page 52. For many states there are two abbreviations for the state name. For example, **Mississippi** can be **MS** or **Miss.** The Post Office encourages the use of the MS form (two capital letters without punctuation).

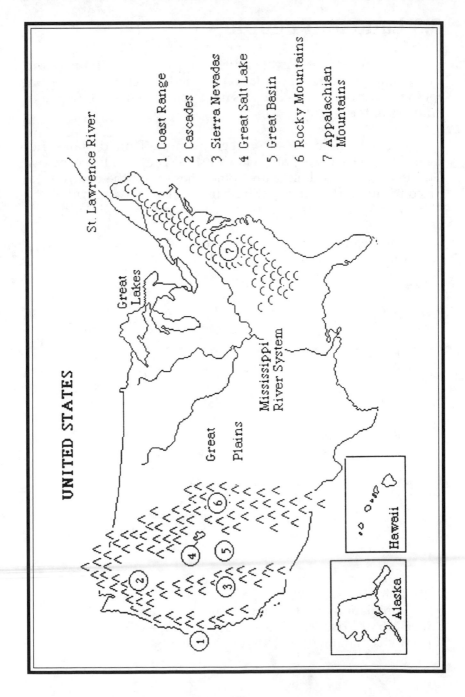

UNITED STATES

St. Lawrence River

Great Lakes

Great Plains

Mississippi River System

Hawaii

Alaska

1 Coast Range
2 Cascades
3 Sierra Nevadas
4 Great Salt Lake
5 Great Basin
6 Rocky Mountains
7 Appalachian Mountains

Land: The United States has an area of 9,371,781 square kilometers. Alaska is the largest state. It is about the same size as Portugal, Spain, France, and Germany together. Alaska is very mountainous. The highest mountain is Denali, which is 6,914 meters high — the highest in North America.

Hawaii is a group of islands in the Pacific Ocean, 3,857 kilometers from California. The islands are actually the tops of volcanoes. Hawaii is one of the smallest states (16,760 square kilometers). It is a little smaller than the country of Kuwait.

The other 48 states stretch across the North American continent for about 4,800 kilometers from the Atlantic to the Pacific. There is a wide variety of land forms; the major features are shown on the physical features map on the facing page. Along the Atlantic Coast the land is flat. Inland from the coast there is a low range of mountains, the Appalachian Mountains. The highest point is Mount Mitchell in North Carolina (2,037 meters).

In the middle of the continent there is the great Mississippi River, which flows south to the Gulf of Mexico, and the Great Lakes and the Saint Lawrence River which flow northeast through Canada to the Atlantic Ocean. The middle part of the country is generally flat, and toward the west, it is very open — from Texas north to the Dakotas this area is called the Great Plains.

The west is mountainous. There are two main mountain systems: The Rocky Mountains and, nearer the Pacific, the Sierra Nevada and the Coast/Cascade Range. In between the mountain ranges is a dry, semidesert area called the Great Basin. Great Salt Lake is in the middle of this basin. The highest mountain in the west is Mount Whitney (4,418 meters) in the Sierra Nevadas of California.

Climate: In general, the climate of the United States is temperate, with four distinct seasons. The northern half of the country usually has snow in the winter. The coldest months are December, January, and February, and the warmest are June, July, and August.

The coldest places are Alaska, Montana, the Dakotas, Minnesota, Wisconsin, northern Michigan, northern New York, and northern New England. The hottest places are the Carolinas, Florida, Georgia, Alabama, Mississippi, Louisiana, Texas, New Mexico, and Arizona.

Southern Florida and Hawaii are sub-tropical. Southern California has a Mediterranean-type climate. The driest areas are southern California, Nevada, Utah, Arizona, New Mexico, and northern Alaska. The East is much wetter than the West, and the wettest areas are in the lower Mississippi basin.

Population: According to the official census of 2000, the population is 281 million. 80.3% of the population lives in metropolitan areas (cities), 19.7% in rural areas (countryside). The largest state is California, with a population of 34 million. Six other states have populations of over 10 million. They are (highest to lowest) Texas, New York, Florida, Illinois, Pennsylvania, and Ohio. The three smallest states have populations of about one-half million each. They are Alaska, Vermont, and Wyoming. For more information, see the Appendix.

In general in recent years, the U.S. population has shifted south and then west. Climate is one reason; economics is another. Industries and the people who work in them have moved from the so-called "rust belt" to the "sun belt." Florida, Texas, and California have grown much faster than such northern industrial states as New York, Pennsylvania, Ohio, and Illinois. Also, in general, the populations of urban areas have grown faster than those of rural areas. At the same time, the populations of the urban areas have shifted from the "inner cities" to the suburbs. Unlike cities in many parts of the world, American cities have centers troubled with poverty and crime, while the surrounding, more open areas are generally wealthier and have fewer social problems.

The largest cities are listed below according to the 2000 census. The metropolitan figures include the smaller cities and towns that are around the city itself.

City, State	City Population	Metropolitan Population
New York, NY	8,008,278	21,199,865
Los Angeles, CA	3,694,820	16,373,645
Chicago, IL	2,896,016	9,157,540
Houston, TX	1,953,631	4,669,571
Philadelphia, PA	1,517,550	6,188,463
Phoenix, AZ	1,321,045	3,251,876
San Diego, CA	1,223,400	2,813,833
Dallas, TX	1,188,580	5,221,801
San Antonio, TX	1,144,646	1,592,383
Detroit, MI	951,270	5,456,428

Language: American English is the dominant language spoken throughout the country. There are dialects in different regions (Northern, Midland, and Southern), but Americans usually do not have any difficulty understanding each other.

In some parts of the United States you will encounter large groups of people who use another language on a daily basis. Spanish is the first language for many people in New York City, Miami, the Southwest, and California. You will find people in northern New England and New York who speak Canadian French. Many Native Americans have their own languages, as do the native people of Alaska and Hawaii. Although most Americans are monolingual, in recent years bilingualism has become more common.

Ethnic Groups: There are many minority ethnic groups in the United States. The largest such group is African Americans, who are about 15% of the population. Spanish-speaking people from Mexico, Puerto Rico, Cuba, and other Hispanic countries are about 13% of the population. Asian Americans are mainly Chinese, Japanese, and Indochinese. They represent about 4% of the U.S. population. Native Americans are a little less than one percent of the total.

3.4 Government

Government operates on three levels in the United States: national, state, and local. The Constitution of the United States outlines the basic principles on which the government is founded, and it describes the powers that belong to federal and state governments.

The **federal government** makes and enforces laws, collects taxes, provides services, and protects the people while working toward national and international security. There are three branches of federal government: executive, legislative, and judicial. The **executive branch** is made up of the President, executive departments, and independent agencies. The President of the United States is responsible for enforcing laws, choosing high government officials, commanding the army, conducting foreign affairs, and recommending laws to Congress. The executive departments are responsible for the administration of the federal government. There are 14 departments: State, Treasury, Defense, Justice, Interior, Agriculture, Commerce, Labor, Health and Human Services, Housing and Urban Development, Transportation, Energy, Education, and Veterans Affairs. The independent agencies help implement and regulate laws. They operate in fields such as nuclear energy, interstate commerce, small business, communications, etc.

The **legislative branch** of the United States government includes Congress (which consists of the Senate and the House of Representatives) and a number of administrative agencies.

Congress makes and changes laws, establishes federal taxes, and decides on funds for operating the federal government. The Senate has 100 members, two from each state. The House of Representatives has 435 members, who are divided among the states according to the number of people living in each state. Distribution of seats in the House is changed every ten years to keep up to date with the country's current population. The largest state, California, has 53 representatives. The seven smallest states have one representative each.

The **judicial branch** of the government consists of the Supreme Court, the highest court in the country, and the federal district courts located throughout the nation. There are also 11 federal appeals courts, which are above the district courts. Federal courts decide cases that involve federal laws and the Constitution.

There are two major political parties in the United States: Democrat and Republican. Most members of government come from one of these two parties, although several minor parties also exist.

National elections are held every two years on the first Tuesday in November. Representatives to Congress are elected every two years, the President and Vice-President are elected every four years, and Senators are elected every six years. The next presidential election is scheduled for 2004. A citizen must be at least 18 years old to vote. (See the Appendix for additional information.)

State governments are similar to the national government. The executive officer is called the governor, and each state has a legislature and a judicial system. State government is important in controlling roads, vehicles and drivers, social welfare programs, public universities, prisons, banking, tourism, and utilities such as electric companies.

Local government can be administered at the county, city, town, or village level. Each state is divided into counties. Counties are important in some states, and less important in others.

The best known county officer is the head of the county police, the sheriff. The highest political officer in a city is called the mayor. The mayor usually works with a small executive advisory group called the city council or aldermen. Each city has its own police force. Town government is similar to city government, but it is smaller and is usually administered by a small committee of community leaders. Cities and towns are responsible for public schools, local streets and roads, water and sewer, and services such as trash/garbage collection, public transportation, public libraries, and recreational facilities. (Incidentally, the public library is a good place to visit. You can learn a lot about the town and meet local people there.)

3.5 Economy

The economy of the United States is based on **free enterprise**. In such a system, individual people and companies are free to make their own economic decisions. They own the raw materials and machinery needed to make their product, and they decide how to market their product in order to make a profit. The federal government is involved in the system by regulating business in certain ways. For instance, it establishes antitrust laws to prevent one company from controlling an entire industry, and laws to prevent environmental pollution.

The United States has many **natural resources**: fuels for energy such as coal, petroleum, and natural gas; rich soil for agriculture; water for agriculture; forests that provide wood for building and paper; and both freshwater and ocean fish.

Manufacturing is the most important economic activity in the country. The leading products are: non-electric machinery, transportation equipment, chemicals, food products, electric and electronic equipment, metal products, primary metals, printed materials, paper, and rubber and plastic products.

3.6 Religion

The Constitution of the United States specifically forbids establishment of a state religion, and its First Amendment guarantees **freedom of religion** for every citizen of the nation. This freedom is one reason that many people have immigrated. As a result, there are many different religions represented. Approximately 60% of the population belong to organized religious groups. Of that number, 52% are Protestant, 37% are Roman Catholic, 4% are Jewish, 4% are Moslem, and 3% are from Eastern Orthodox Churches. The largest Protestant groups in the country are: Baptist, United Methodist, Presbyterian, Lutheran, and Episcopalian.

Although there are a variety of religious groups in the United States, Christian traditions have influenced the country the most. All offices are closed on Sundays, and many holidays are based on Christian tradition (see section 2.14).

3.7 Education

Education in the United States is based on the belief that learning how to think for oneself through research and problem-solving skills is more important than learning fact.

Education is guaranteed to all children from the age of 5 through 18 in the public school system. Public schools are funded with money from taxes, so parents do not pay a specific additional charge when their children attend a public school. Other types of schools are parochial and private schools. **Parochial schools** are funded by religious denominations, and children attending those schools usually pay some additional fees. **Private schools** are self-supporting and are therefore the most expensive.

Americans often begin their education at a public or private nursery school when they are 2, 3, or 4 years old. Nursery schools give children a chance to learn to play with other children and to begin learning skills that will help them in school. Most students then go to local public schools for a year or two of kindergarten,

 followed by elementary school (sometimes called grade school, grammar school, or primary school). They are required by law to start in first grade at age 6. After elementary school, students attend middle school or junior high school and then high school. In all, they spend 12 years in elementary, middle school, and high school (also called **secondary school**). These schools are controlled by locally elected school boards.

After high school, there are a number of different types of institutions that offer higher education. Community colleges provide two years of higher education at minimal cost. State colleges and universities provide the four years of education needed to receive a bachelor's degree; these two- and four-year programs are called **undergraduate education**. The universities also have graduate schools that offer additional education for a master's degree and/or a doctorate. Fees vary from state to state. In addition to tax-supported community and state (public) institutions, there are also many private colleges and universities. They are usually more expensive than public institutions.

3.8 The Arts

In general, the arts in America have been influenced by three traditions: European, Native American, and African. The unique American experience of exploring and developing a new continent has also influenced the arts.

The decorative traditions of Native American art are still seen in many ways, especially in weaving and pottery. These traditions existed before the arrival of European explorers. The American Southwest is the contemporary center of this tradition.

Many settlers from Europe arrived during the seventeenth and eighteenth centuries. They brought their artistic traditions with them. Many artists and craftsmen, however, produced distinctive American art forms that are called Colonial (early 1600s to late 1700s) and Federalist (late 1700s to early 1800s). Especially well known are the furniture and household furnishings of these times. Americans are also very proud of the architecture of this period. Many buildings have been preserved and restored. The U.S. government now protects approximately 1,800 national historic landmarks, and many other government and private organizations protect other architectural and historic sites. In some places villages have been restored or rebuilt. Some of the best known are Williamsburg in Virginia, Sturbridge Village and Plymouth Plantation in Massachusetts, and Strawbery Banke in New Hampshire. One famous house in Boston, Massachusetts, is the home of Paul Revere, a hero of the revolution and a great silversmith.

During the nineteenth century, American literature began speaking in a voice different from English literature. The American wilderness and frontier, along with American ideas of freedom and independence, contributed in important ways to writers who are still well known. James Fenimore Cooper was America's first popular novelist. He wrote novels about the frontier, such as *The Last of the Mohicans*. Ralph Waldo Emerson and Henry David Thoreau were essayists who celebrated American self-reliance and independent thinking. Herman Melville's *Moby Dick* stands as one of the classics of world literature. On one level, it is a battle of man against nature — the hunt for the great white whale. Walt Whitman became America's first great poet, with the notion of democracy as one of his central themes. In 1884, Mark Twain published his masterpiece, *Huckleberry Finn*, perhaps the most important American novel ever written. But the most powerful novel of the nineteenth century was *Uncle Tom's Cabin*, written by Harriet Beecher Stowe in 1852. It brought international attention to the evils of slavery, and it is often called one of the causes of the American Civil War.

The African American experience has been the most important influence on music in America. In the nineteenth century, African Americans developed religious songs called **spirituals**. These choral songs, based on African call-and-response patterns, led to a variety of musical forms, from gospel music to blues and

jazz. The **jazz** of African Americans is a unique contribution to the music of the contemporary world, from pop to rock to classical music.

In the fields of painting and sculpture, American artists tended to work within the European tradition. Some artists produced work with distinctively American themes. Thomas Cole was the first important landscape painter in the United States. He founded the **Hudson River School** (1820–1850). Artists in this school portrayed American forests, rivers, and mountains in romantic scenes. In the twentieth century, a group of regional painters, sometimes called **anti-modernists**, tried to portray the strength and energy of rural America. Thomas Hart Benton of Missouri was one of the most successful artists of the 1930s.

There are over 7,000 art museums in the United States. Many of these museums have special collections of American art. The most important collections can be seen in the Los Angeles County Museum, the Chicago Art Institute, the Butler Institute in Youngstown, Ohio, the Philadelphia Museum of Art, the Boston Museum of Fine Arts, the Smithsonian Institution in Washington, D.C., and, in New York City, the Metropolitan Museum of Art, the Museum of Modern Art, and the Whitney Museum of American Art.

Throughout the twentieth century, American writers, musicians, painters, sculptors, craftsmen, and architects continued to find ways to express both the diversity and the unity of the American experience. Two art forms stand out among all others: the cinema and the skyscraper. The cinema, popularly called the **movies**, along with its cousin, television, dominates mass entertainment on a worldwide basis. The **skyscraper** dominates the skyline of America's cities as a symbol of America as the most powerful country in the world. As a symbol, the skyscrapers of the World Trade Center in New York City became the target of terrorism.

3.9 Technology and Change

The United States has been profoundly shaped and changed by technological developments.

In the 19th century, the development of the **railroad** was a significant factor in the development of the continent. In 1869, the east and west coasts were linked by an intercontinental railway. From that time on, more and more Americans looked to the "Golden West" as a new frontier. The lives of the Native Americans of the West were changed forever.

Late in the 19th century, Thomas Edison invented the light bulb. The day no longer ended with sunset, and the resulting **electrification** of the country intensified the great industrial revolution of the 19th century. The American family, and especially American women, began to enjoy dozens of labor-saving devices such as the electric refrigerator and the dishwasher.

Possibly, the most profound development of the 20th century was Henry Ford's mass production of the **automobile** in 1908. The roads of America developed, culminating in the Interstate Highway System. Cities changed as suburbs grew. The trucking industry replaced the railroad in importance. The auto industry of Detroit became a significant part of the American economy. And the people of America became a population on wheels, moving freely to new jobs, homes, and communities. Soon after the automobile came **aviation**, launched by the Wright Brothers in 1903. Eventually, every city in the country could be reached in just a few hours.

On the international scene, the development of the **atomic bomb**, for better or worse, has certainly dominated world politics and has made the United States a world superpower.

Beginning in the 1950s, the development of **television** ("TV") caused a great change in the way families lived their daily lives and in the way individuals viewed the world. Debate over the positive and negative impacts of TV is a discussion that is still going on.

Most recently, the **computer** and its attendant capacities, e-mail, and the internet, have become a part of life for more and more businesses, families, and individuals. The long-term effect of the computer is still not completely understood, but many people would say that a person who has not become computer-literate is no longer part of mainstream America.

Many technological innovations have grown out of America's and other countries' exploration of space. **Satellites** monitor the weather and make worldwide communication possible. The **space shuttle** has helped launch hundreds of these satellites. Now America, Russia, and their allies are building a **space station** that will stimulate new technologies for the future benefit of people all over the earth.

Appendix: The 50 States

This list of the 50 states and the federal District of Columbia emphasizes the connection between politics and population. Population figures are based on 2000 census and are rounded to the nearest 1,000.

Electoral votes are used for presidential elections only. The candidate who gets the most votes in a state wins all the electoral votes of that state. The electoral vote is based on the number of senators and representatives from that state. Each state has two senators. The number of representatives is determined by the population of the state.

As a result of the 2000 census, California, with the largest population, will have 53 representatives and thus 55 electoral votes. The number of representatives and the electoral vote may change in the year 2010 when the next census is taken. The census is taken every ten years and has been since 1790.

(R) signifies Republican Party, (D) stands for Democratic Party, and (I) means Independent.

1. California. Capital: Sacramento
Population: 33,827,000
Electoral Votes: 55
2000 vote: Gore
Senators: Feinstein (D), Boxer (D)

2. Texas. Capital: Austin
Population: 20,852,000
Electoral Votes: 34
2000 vote: Bush
Senators: Hutchison (R), Gramm (R)

3. New York. Capital: Albany
Population: 18,976,000
Electoral Votes: 31
2000 vote: Gore
Senators: Clinton (D), Schumer (D)

4. Florida. Capital: Tallahassee
Population: 15,982,000
Electoral Votes: 27
2000 vote: Bush
Senators: Nelson (D), Graham (D)

5. Illinois. Capital: Springfield
Population: 12,419,000
Electoral Votes: 21
2000 vote: Gore
Senators: Durbin (D), Fitzgerald (R)

6. Pennsylvania. Capital: Harrisburg
Population: 12,281,000
Electoral Votes: 21
2000 vote: Gore
Senators: Santorum (R), Specter (R)

7. Ohio. Capital: Columbus
Population: 11,353,000
Electoral Votes: 20
2000 vote: Bush
Senators: DeWine (R), Voinovich (R)

8. Michigan. Capital: Lansing
Population: 9,938,000
Electoral Votes: 17
2000 vote: Gore
Senators: Stabenow (D), Levin (D)

9. New Jersey. Capital: Trenton
Population: 8,414,000
Electoral Votes: 15
2000 vote: Gore
Senators: Corzine (D), Torricelli (D)

10. Georgia. Capital: Atlanta
Population: 8,186,000
Electoral Votes: 15
2000 vote: Bush
Senators: Cleland (D), Miller (D)

11. North Carolina. Capital: Raleigh
Population: 8,049,000
Electoral Votes: 15
2000 vote: Bush
Senators: Edwards (D), Helms (R)

12. Virginia. Capital: Richmond
Population: 7,079,000
Electoral Votes: 13
2000 vote: Bush
Senators: Allen (R), Warner (R)

13. Massachusetts. Capital: Boston
Population: 6,349,000
Electoral Votes: 12
2000 vote: Gore
Senators: Kennedy (D), Kerry (D)

14. Indiana. Capital: Indianapolis
Population: 6,080,000
Electoral Votes: 11
2000 vote: Bush
Senators: Lugar (R), Bayh (D)

15. Washington. Capital: Olympia
Population: 5,894,000
Electoral Votes: 11
2000 vote: Gore
Senators: Cantwell (D), Murray (D)

16. Tennessee. Capital: Nashville
Population: 5,689,000
Electoral Votes: 11
2000 vote: Bush
Senators: Frist (R), Thompson (R)

17. Missouri. Capital: Jefferson City
Population: 5,595,000
Electoral Votes: 11
2000 vote: Bush
Senators: Carnahan (D), Bond (R)

18. Wisconsin. Capital: Madison
Population: 5,364,000
Electoral Votes: 10
2000 vote: Gore
Senators: Kohl (D), Feingold (D)

19. Maryland. Capital: Annapolis
Population: 5,296,000
Electoral Votes: 10
2000 vote: Gore
Senators: Sarbanes (D), Mikulski (D)

20. Arizona. Capital: Phoenix
Population: 5,131,000
Electoral Votes: 10
2000 vote: Bush
Senators: Kyl (R), McCain (R)

21. Minnesota. Capital: St. Paul
Population: 4,919,000
Electoral Votes: 10
2000 vote: Gore
Senators: Dayton (D), Wellstone (D)

22. Louisiana. Capital: Baton Rouge
Population: 4,469,000
Electoral Votes: 9
2000 vote: Bush
Senators: Landrieu (D), Breaux (D)

23. Alabama. Capital: Montgomery
Population: 4,447,000
Electoral Votes: 9
2000 vote: Bush
Senators: Sessions (R), Shelby (R)

24. Colorado. Capital: Denver
Population: 4,301,000
Electoral Votes: 9
2000 vote: Bush
Senators: Allard (R), Campbell (R)

25. Kentucky. Capital: Frankfort
Population: 4,042,000
Electoral Votes: 8
2000 vote: Bush
Senators: McConnell (R), Bunning (R)

26. South Carolina. Capital: Columbia
Population: 4,012,000
Electoral Votes: 8
2000 vote: Bush
Senators: Thurmond (R), Hollings (D)

27. Oklahoma. Capital: Oklahoma City
Population: 3,451,000
Electoral Votes: 7
2000 vote: Bush
Senators: Inhofe (R), Nickles (R)

28. Oregon. Capital: Salem
Population: 3,421,000
Electoral Votes: 7
2000 vote: Gore
Senators: Smith (R), Wyden (D)

29. Connecticut. Capital: Hartford
Population: 3,406,000
Electoral Votes: 7
2000 vote: Gore
Senators: Lieberman (D), Dodd (D)

30. Iowa. Capital: Des Moines
Population: 2,926,000
Electoral Votes: 7
2000 vote: Gore
Senators: Harkin (D), Grassley (R)

31. Mississippi. Capital: Jackson
Population: 2,845,000
Electoral Votes: 6
2000 vote: Bush
Senators: Lott (R), Cochran (R)

32. Kansas. Capital: Topeka
Population: 2,688,000
Electoral Votes: 6
2000 vote: Bush
Senators: Roberts (R), Brownback (R)

33. Arkansas. Capital: Little Rock
Population: 2,673,000
Electoral Votes: 6
2000 vote: Bush
Senators: Hutchinson (R), Lincoln (D)

34. Utah. Capital: Salt Lake City
Population: 2,233,000
Electoral Votes: 5
2000 vote: Bush
Senators: Hatch (R), Bennett (R)

35. Nevada. Capital: Carson City
Population: 1,998,000
Electoral Votes: 5
2000 vote: Bush
Senators: Ensign (R), Reid (D)

36. New Mexico. Capital: Santa Fe
Population: 1,819,000
Electoral Votes: 5
2000 vote: Gore
Senators: Bingaman (D), Domenici (R)

37. West Virginia. Capital: Charleston
Population: 1,803,000
Electoral Votes: 5
2000 vote: Bush
Senators: Byrd (D), Rockefeller (D)

38. Nebraska. Capital: Lincoln
Population: 1,711,000
Electoral Votes: 5
2000 vote: Bush
Senators: Nelson (D), Hagel (D)

39. Idaho. Capital: Boise
Population: 1,294,000
Electoral Votes: 4
2000 vote: Bush
Senators: Craig (R), Crapo (R)

40. Maine. Capital: Augusta
Population: 1,275,000
Electoral Votes: 4
2000 vote: Gore
Senators: Snowe (R), Collins (R)

41. New Hampshire. Capital: Concord
Population: 1,236,000
Electoral Votes: 4
2000 vote: Bush
Senators: Smith (R), Gregg (R)

42. Hawaii. Capital: Honolulu
Population: 1,212,000
Electoral Votes: 4
2000 vote: Gore
Senators: Akaka (D), Inouye (D)

43. Rhode Island. Capital: Providence
Population: 1,048,000
Electoral Votes: 4
2000 vote: Gore
Senators: Chafee (R), Reed (D)

44. Montana. Capital: Helena
Population: 902,000
Electoral Votes: 3
2000 vote: Bush
Senators: Burns (R), Baucus (D)

45. Delaware. Capital: Dover
Population: 784,000
Electoral Votes: 3
2000 vote: Gore
Senators: Biden (D), Carper (D)

46. South Dakota. Capital: Pierre
Population: 755,000
Electoral Votes: 3
2000 vote: Bush
Senators: Johnson (D), Daschle (D)

47. North Dakota. Capital: Bismarck
Population: 642,000
Electoral Votes: 3
2000 vote: Bush
Senators: Conrad (D), Dorgan (D)

48. Alaska. Capital: Juneau
Population: 627,000
Electoral Votes: 3
2000 vote: Bush
Senators: Stevens (R), Murkowski (R)

49. Vermont. Capital: Montpelier
Population: 609,000
Electoral Votes: 3
2000 vote: Gore
Senators: Jeffords (I), Leahy (D)

50. Wyoming. Capital: Cheyenne
Population: 494,000
Electoral Votes: 3
2000 vote: Bush
Senators: Thomas (R), Enzi (R)

District of Columbia. (USA Capital)
Population: 572,000
Electoral Votes: 3
2000 vote: Gore

Also Available
from Pro Lingua Associates

Living in France
Living in Italy
Living in Japan
Living in Mexico
Living in Spain
Living in South Korea

American Holidays
Exploring Traditions, Customs, and Backgrounds
by Barbara Klebanow and Sara Fischer

Potluck
Exploring American Foods and Meals
by Raymond C. Clark

Celebrating American Heroes
13 plays for Students of English
Heroes from American History
A Content-Based Reader – 16 Biographies
by Anne Siebert and Raymond C. Clark

Pearls of Wisdom
African and Caribbean Folktales
Student text, Workbook, Cassettes
by Raouf Mama and Mary Romney

Story Cards
North American Indian Tales
by Susannah J. Clark

Rhymes 'n Rhythms
Poems for the ESL Classroom
Student text and Cassette
by Lisa Tenuta